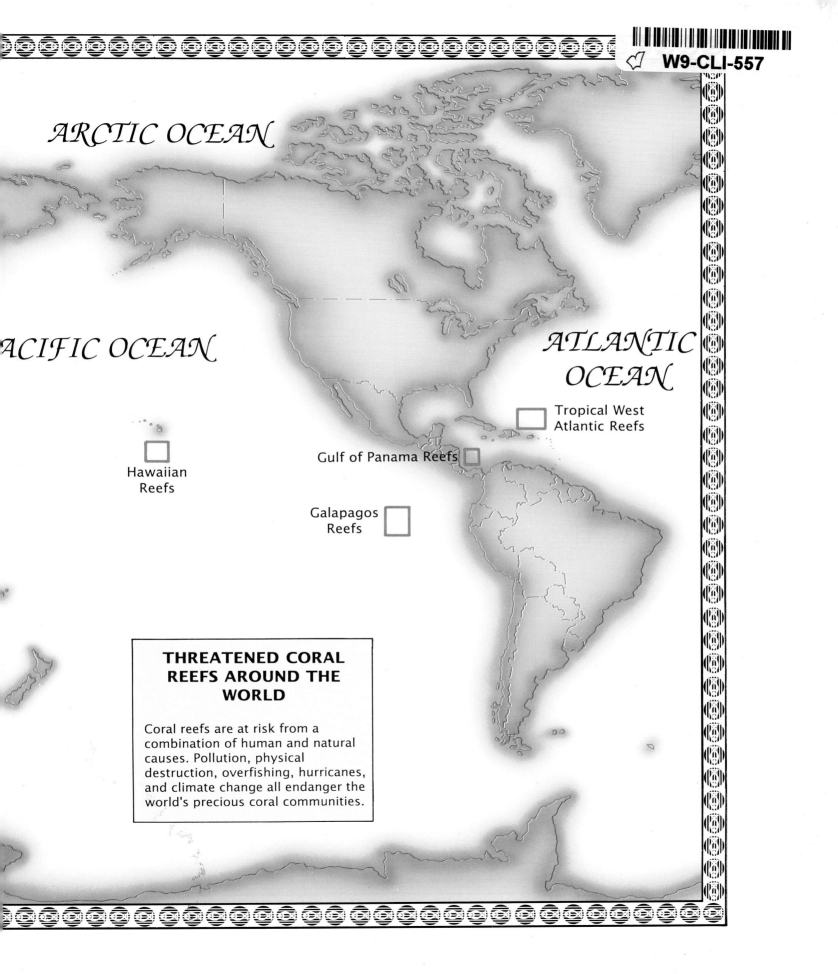

ARCTIC OCEAN

PACIFIC OCEAN

ATLANTIC OCEAN

☐ Tropical West Atlantic Reefs

Gulf of Panama Reefs ☐

☐ Hawaiian Reefs

Galapagos Reefs ☐

THREATENED CORAL REEFS AROUND THE WORLD

Coral reefs are at risk from a combination of human and natural causes. Pollution, physical destruction, overfishing, hurricanes, and climate change all endanger the world's precious coral communities.

THE RED SEA

Kenneth Mallory

A New England Aquarium Book

FRANKLIN WATTS

New York ○ London ○ Toronto ○ Sydney

1991

The author would especially like to thank Dr. Les Kaufman for his helpful critique and Paul Erickson for most of the beautiful photographs that accompany the text. Many of the ideas here are based on an International Union for Conservation of Nature and Natural Resources (IUCN) book entitled *Key Environments, Red Sea,* published by Pergamon Press. Thanks are due to Carol Fiore of the New England Aquarium's education department. And thanks also go to the New England Aquarium for helping to make this and other books like it possible.

Frontispiece: A school of small, big-eyed nocturnal fishes, called sweepers, swim through a garden of soft coral.

Maps by Vantage Art, Inc.

Page 4: photograph copyright © NASA
Pages 9, 30 left & bottom right, 31: photographs copyright © Jeff Rotman
Page 23: photograph copyright © Peter Arnold Inc. by Norbert Wu
Pages 28 inset, 30 top right: photographs copyright © Chris Newbert
All other photographs copyright © 1988 New England Aquarium by Paul Erickson

Library of Congress Cataloging-in-Publication Data

Mallory, Kenneth.
The Red Sea / by Kenneth Mallory.
p.   cm.
"A New England Aquarium book."
Includes bibliographical references and index.
Summary: Examines the animal and plant life and coral reefs of the Red Sea.
ISBN 531-15213-8—0-531-10993-3 (lib. bdg.)
1. Marine biology—Red Sea—Juvenile literature.   2. Marine flora—Red Sea—Juvenile literature.   [1. Marine animals—Red Sea.
2. Marine plants—Red Sea.]   I. Title.
QH94.3.M32   1991
574.92'733—dc20   90-47646 CIP AC

Contents

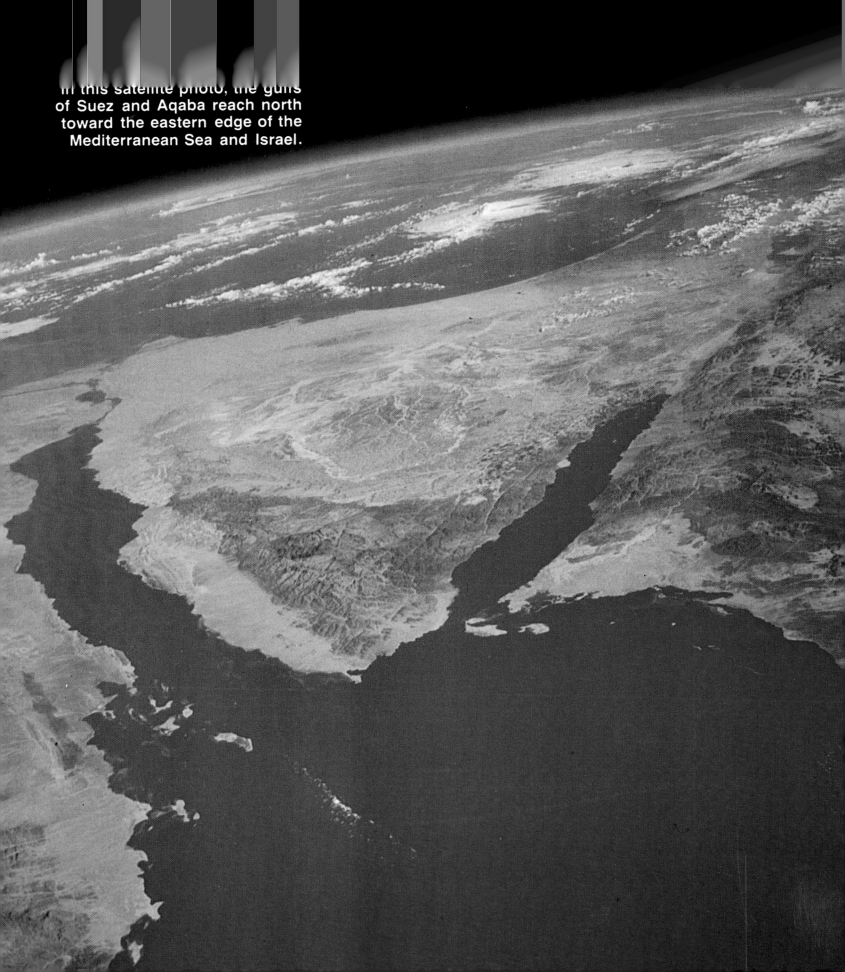

In this satellite photo, the gulfs of Suez and Aqaba reach north toward the eastern edge of the Mediterranean Sea and Israel.

INTRODUCTION

Seen from space, the Red Sea resembles a giant blue garden slug crawling across desert sands to take a drink from the Mediterranean Sea. As the map on page 6 shows, the slug's left antenna represents the Gulf of Suez; its right antenna is the Gulf of Aqaba. At the tip of the Gulf of Suez, the Red Sea connects with the Mediterranean Sea at the Suez Canal. One thousand, three hundred miles (2,093 km) to the south, it flows into the Indian Ocean between Africa and India.

No one really knows how the Red Sea got its name. Some say that at sundown, the surrounding hills of desert sand cast a rosy color on the sea. Others say the name comes from blooms of red algae that scientists call the red tide.

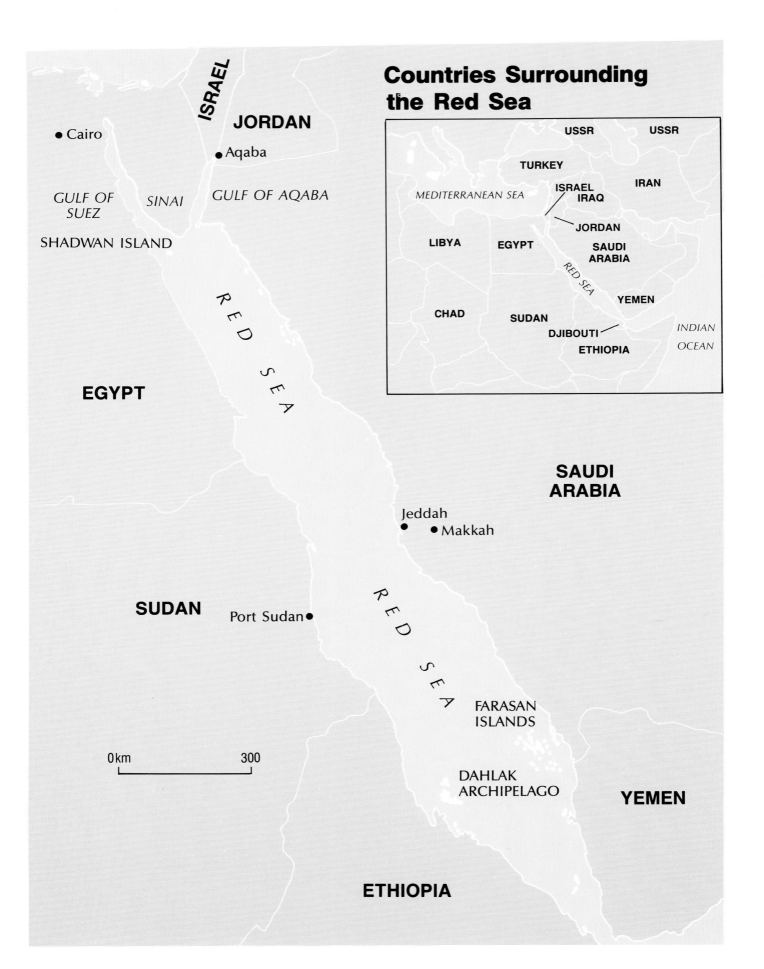

Countries Surrounding the Red Sea

ISRAEL

JORDAN

• Cairo

• Aqaba

GULF OF SUEZ

SINAI

GULF OF AQABA

SHADWAN ISLAND

R E D   S E A

EGYPT

SAUDI ARABIA

Jeddah

• Makkah

SUDAN

Port Sudan •

R E D   S E A

FARASAN ISLANDS

0 km   300

DAHLAK ARCHIPELAGO

YEMEN

ETHIOPIA

USSR   USSR

TURKEY

MEDITERRANEAN SEA

ISRAEL

IRAN

IRAQ

JORDAN

LIBYA   EGYPT

SAUDI ARABIA

RED SEA

YEMEN

CHAD   SUDAN

DJIBOUTI

INDIAN OCEAN

ETHIOPIA

A CHANGING SEA

The Red Sea, which today is about the size of the state of California, is growing at a pace of nearly half an inch (1cm) a year. One could say the Red Sea is an ocean in the making. Thousands of feet below its quiet surface is a boiling pot of volcanic activity. As heat from the Earth's core escapes through cracks in the Red Sea floor, its energy literally pushes the seabed apart at the seams. As the seabed stretches, so does the distance between the continents that border it—Africa to the west and Asia to the east. This process has been going on for millions of years. In 200 million years, the Red Sea might be as wide as the Atlantic Ocean!

The Red Sea has had a history of changing connections with the Mediterranean Sea and the Indian Ocean. Between 5 and 25 million years ago, only the Red and Mediterannean seas were connected. Then, 5 million years ago, an uplifting of the Earth's crust closed the Mediterranean water bridge, but opened a passage to the Indian Ocean to the south. The great period of ice caps and glaciers followed. These ice caps acted like giant sponges that absorbed water from the oceans and seas. During this glacial period—between 2 million and 10,000 years ago—the sea levels dropped so much that the Red Sea was nearly separated from the Indian Ocean again.

This history of on-again, off-again connections with larger oceans and seas has given the Red Sea a special character of its own. Its occasional isolation has given rise to a number of plant and animal species that can be found nowhere else.

In 1859 the French builder Ferdinand de Lesseps and his company built a miracle of engineering—the Suez Canal (see page 8). What nature had closed off 5 million years before, humans now reopened after ten years of hard labor. Water could now flow continuously between the Mediterranean Sea's Port Said in Egypt and the Red Sea's Port Bûr Taufîq at the Gulf of Suez.

Oil tankers and cargo boats weren't the only passengers through the locks of the canal. As many as thirty different kinds of fishes

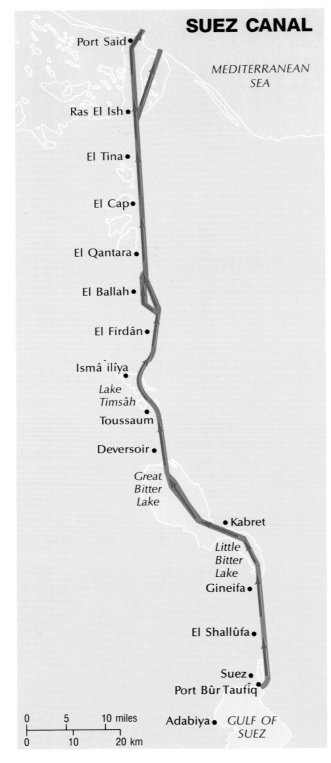

SUEZ CANAL

Port Said•

MEDITERRANEAN SEA

Ras El Ish•

El Tina•

El Cap•

El Qantara•

El Ballah•

El Firdân•

Ismâ ilîya•

Lake Timsâh

Toussaum•

Deversoir•

Great Bitter Lake

• Kabret

Little Bitter Lake

Gineifa•

El Shallûfa•

Suez•
Port Bûr Taufîq•

Adabiya• *GULF OF SUEZ*

0   5   10 miles
0   10   20 km

made the journey between the two seas as well. Water flows northward through the Suez Canal, which may have helped many of the fishes to migrate from the Red Sea to the Mediterranean. Because fewer kinds of fishes live in the eastern Mediterranean, Red Sea fishes may stand a better chance to find different sources of food. And because the waters of the Suez Canal and the surrounding Bitter Lakes are so salty, only salt-tolerant Red Sea fishes could adjust, at least at first. Not surprisingly, a species of the adaptable killifish was one of the first to make it to the Mediterranean.

Today some of the most important fishes sold in Mediterranean markets are migrants from the Red Sea through the Suez Canal. Goatfish, lizardfish and rabbitfish, and even the Red Sea barracuda are valuable fishery catches along the coast of Israel. Halfbeaks, silversides, and pony-

The Suez Canal forged a waterway that linked the Mediterranean Sea with the Gulf of Suez, prompting the northward migration of certain fishes from the Red Sea. The journey wasn't easy, however, since the fishes had to travel through salty waters and man-made locks before reaching the Mediterranean Sea.

Reptilian-looking lizardfishes such as these have migrated from the Red Sea through the Suez Canal to the Mediterranean Sea, where they have become commercially important as food fishes.

fish are new arrivals in the Mediterranean, too. In comparison only about five or six kinds of Mediterranean fishes, among them the sea bass and mullet, have made it through the Suez locks to face the fierce competition and predators that await them in the Red Sea.

THE CORAL REEF

Red Sea water is saltier than any ocean in the world. It is also extremely warm. The summer surface temperatures in the Gulf of Aqaba, for example, can be a bathtub 80 to 90 degrees Fahrenheit (26.7–32.2 degrees C). Despite such extreme temperatures and saltiness, beneath the surface of the Red Sea lies a garden of underwater treasures—the coral reef.

It takes thousands of years to build a coral reef. Like most coral reefs around the world, Red Sea reefs are formed by millions of

Six divers appear at the surface of the Red Sea as a seventh expedition member in a rubber inflatable raft moves in to help. The reef they are exploring lies just below them.

(Below) The camera looks up through a garden of soft coral and a shimmering school of orange fairy basslet fishes. A hovering diver seems strangely out of place in this underwater world.

A school of sweepers swarms through branches of soft coral. Such big-eyed fishes are usually more active at night.

marine animals called polyps. Polyps remain in one place and use tentacles to capture and eat tiny animals called zooplankton that drift by. But polyps also depend on microscopic algae that live buried in the soft tissue of their bodies. Like plants, the tiny algae, or zooxanthellae, use the energy of the sun to produce food. These zooxanthellae share the food with their host, the coral polyp. Without nourishment from their algae, many coral animals would die, and none would grow very quickly. Corals that live in caves and deep water, where there is little light and no zooxanthellae, grow slowly and are usually quite small.

A polyp of one of the reef's many kinds of stony corals extends its tentacles from its protective limestone cup in search of food.

A coral polyp forms a cuplike skeleton by converting the calcium in seawater into solid limestone. Most kinds of polyps live together in colonies that form unusual shapes like bushes, boulders, pillars, tables, or dinner plates. As the polyps grow, they continue to make new limestone skeletons on top of the old ones they leave behind.

Reefs also provide a home for another kind of coral called soft corals. Sea fans and sea whips are soft corals whose skeletons are composed of a flexible material that looks and feels like the stem of a plant. Other kinds of soft corals collapse into rubbery buttons or formless mounds of leathery jelly if they are removed from the water. Besides the water pressure inside their bodies, tiny needles

(Right) This kind of soft coral forms huge basketlike nets that stretch into the waters around the reef. (Below) Stony corals form colonies of thousands of animals in the shape of yellow-edged plates. Orange fairy basslets hover above to look for food.

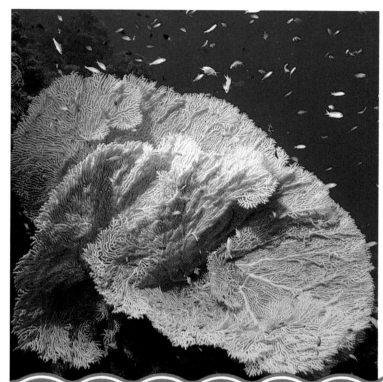

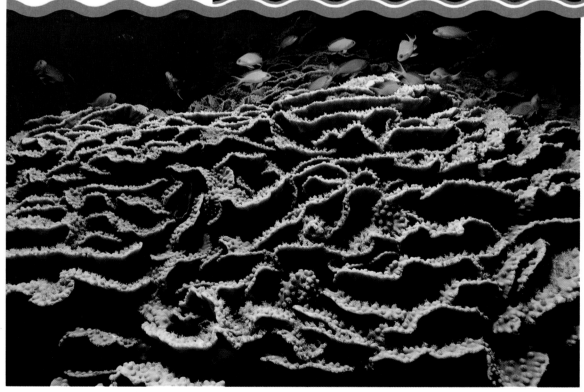

Many of the reef's colors come from gardens of soft corals.

of limestone buried inside the soft corals' tissues help to give them support. These needles act rather like the poles of a pup tent. They allow soft corals to bend with the flow of currents and wave-tossed waters.

At a depth of forty feet (12.2m), fishes and other sea animals flock to branches of soft coral that resemble miniature trees. On a Red Sea reef soft corals display a rainbow of colors you may not find on any other reef. Soft corals can live in places where many stony corals cannot survive, such as cave openings and on steep rocky walls that drop hundreds of feet. That is because they don't depend on sunlight for food the way most stony corals do.

(Facing page) Soft coral polyps extend thousands of tentacles to feed on a thick soup of floating plankton animals. A longnose hawkfish (bottom, right) takes refuge in one of the coral branches.

FISHES OF THE REEF:
Feeding and Breeding

Fishes poke in and out of limestone walls that form the structure of the reef. Among the branches of soft coral gardens they gather in schools so thick that they block the sun. Here they look for food and protection from predators. And that's not always so easy in a sea with over a thousand different kinds of fishes.

One mystery of the Red Sea is how so many similar species live side by side. But similar species may not be so similar after all. Al-

Schools of fishes are sometimes so large that they can block out the sun.

**A solitary bannerfish swims with a Red Sea
grouper among the corals of the reef. This
species of bannerfish is found in the Red Sea
and the Gulf of Aden, and nowhere else.**

though they look remarkably alike, the Red Sea bannerfish and its close cousin, the pennantfish, are rarely seen feeding in the same part of the reef. The bannerfish grazes on worms and other tiny animals that crawl on the surface of the reef. By swimming some distance away, the pennantfish gobbles tiny mid-water zooplankton that swarm in the water above the reef.

The bannerfish is one of over 100 kinds of fishes that live in the Red Sea and nowhere else. The pennantfish can be found as far away as Australia. But the Red Sea bannerfish lives only in the Red Sea and in the nearby Gulf of Aden.

Other kinds of fishes that live only in the Red Sea include the blue-cheeked and the exquisite butterflyfishes. Often seen in pairs and sometimes in small groups, the blue-cheeked butterflyfish prefers the reef's night life. During the day they hang around coral ledges trying not to attract attention. Being a nighttime specialist may help them avoid competition for food with their exquisite butterflyfish cousins. The exquisite butterflyfish feeds on the tips of coral polyps. Corals produce a slimy mucous coating that some fishes eat as if it were a delicious pudding.

(Above) Another example of a fish found only in the Red Sea, the masked butterfly fish is posed against a background of a coral reef. (Facing page) The map angelfish (top) gets its name from the large yellow patch of color on its body that resembles the outline of a map. (Bottom) Adult emperor angelfish like this one feed mainly on sponges.

Fishes that eat coral polyps can endanger a coral reef, but that's rarely a problem for most corals. Fishes and crabs often nibble pieces of coral polyps instead of eating them whole. Some even defend their coral colonies against fearsome threats, such as the crown-of-thorns sea star.

Swarms of hungry crown-of-thorns sea stars can blanket a reef. First they turn their stomachs inside out and push them out through their mouths. Then they let their stomachs' juices digest the polyps smothered below. Scientists now think their population explosions are part of a natural process. By eating the coral polyps, the crown-of-thorns open space on the reef that become new homes for other kinds of corals.

The crown-of-thorns sea star has an appetite for living coral polyps. If enough of them graze together, they can create white patches of dead coral throughout the reef.

Parrotfish eat algae on the surface of limestone rock, but they often scrape off coral pieces as well.

As you can see, a coral polyp's protective limestone house isn't always a guarantee of safety. And animals that like to eat coral are by no means limited to the butterflyfishes and the crown-of-thorns sea star. Brightly colored parrotfish prowl the reef with their powerful beaklike teeth, which they use to scrape coral rock. One Red Sea species, the bumphead parrotfish, prefers live coral. Other kinds of parrotfish are after the algae or plants on the rock surface. Whole patches of living coral are sometimes ground up in the process. But the fish make up for this damage to the reef by grinding coral into sand. The sand then can help fill in cracks in the reef to make it even stronger.

One kind of Red Sea fish with an impressive set of teeth is the Napoleon, or humphead, wrasse. Considered the giant of the wrasse family, these fish can measure as long as 6 feet (2 m). The humphead wrasses have special sets of grinding teeth so powerful they can crack the shell of a sea urchin or cowrie to eat the animal inside. Luckily for the coral reef, the wrasse hasn't developed an appetite for coral.

No dive to a Red Sea coral reef would be complete without an encounter with black damselfish defending its undersea garden. The black damselfish fears neither shark nor human intruder. By its constant nip-and-run tactics, it protects a "lawn" of thin filamentlike algae from being browsed by other species. As the one who trims (nibbles) the lawn, the spirited little damsel (measuring up to 4 to 5 inches [10.2 to 12.7 cm]) has a constant source of food.

The long humphead wrasse swims off toward another part of the reef.

While some fishes are daytime gardeners, others find their food at night. When the sun goes down, many of the brightly colored animals we see in the Red Sea during the day retire to their hiding places on the reef. They are replaced by a new set of animals specifically equipped for prowling in the dark.

Some fishes have large saucer eyes with a special lining at the back of the eye called a tapetum. The tapetum is especially developed in soldier-, cardinal-, and squirrelfishes' eyes. Light first passes through the lens to the retina and then hits the lining, which reflects it back to the retina. This doubling of the light helps nighttime hunters find shrimp and other kinds of food that come out under cover of the dark.

The flashlight fish has solved the problem of night vision with a set of built-in headlights. It relies on bioluminescence, a chemical process that produces light. Millions of tiny bacteria that live just be-

The half-moon bioluminescent organs of the Red Sea flashlight fish enable it to see and attract food, and to communicate with other flashlight fish.

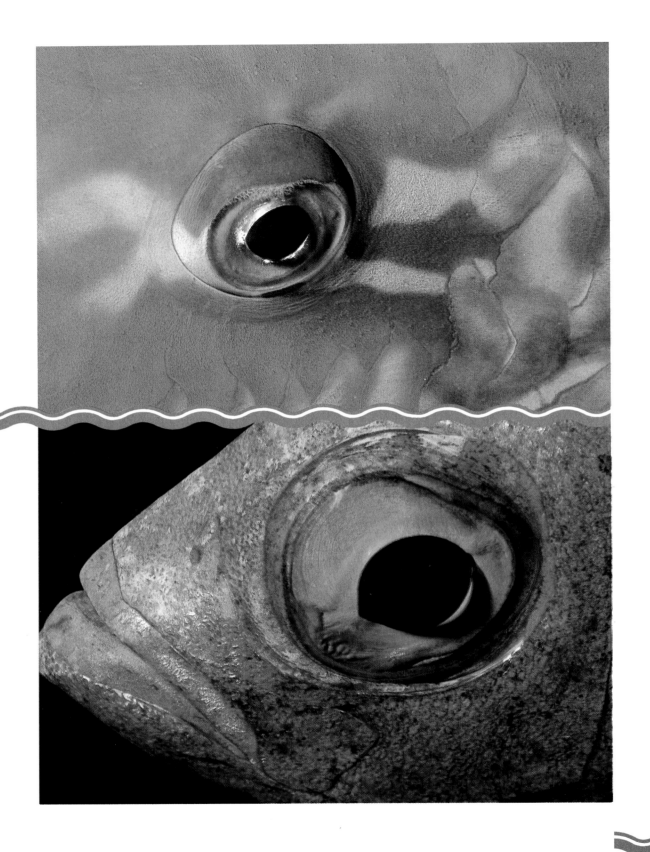

low the flashlight fish's eyes are packed into two organs the shape of half moons. The fish's blood brings these glowing bacteria oxygen and food for energy.

Like the firefly, flashlight fish can blink on and off. The one kind of flashlight fish in the Red Sea has a fold of skin beneath each eye. When the fish wants to turn its headlight off, it raises its lids like a shade, but in reverse. The light from a flashlight fish's eyes is so strong that it can hunt and navigate with it. By turning its lights on and off, flashlight fish may confuse hungry predators, signal to a mate, or attract zooplankton as its prey. Red Sea flashlight fish come into shallow water to feed at night. When they do, the whole seashore glows with their light.

Along with finding food, other major survival activities of reef animals are finding mates and safeguarding their young. For protection, eggs sometimes develop entirely inside the mother, sometimes even inside the father. Some parents cast eggs into ocean currents by the millions and never see them again. Others wrap their eggs in a form of protective jelly that even the hungriest animal will avoid. But one of the most unusual stories of reproduction in the Red Sea is about the swarms of fish called fairy basslets.

Fairy basslets live in huge groups consisting of a single, large, reddish purple male and a harem of orange females. What advantage can this provide for the fairy basslet? Biologists think the creation of a carefully controlled territory, a patch of the reef for example, helps protect the group as a whole. The close grouping of a harem also allows many different females—fertilized by the lone male—to bear young.

(Facing page) The eye of a parrotfish (top), not a nightime prowler, has the same exotic design as the rest of its body. (Bottom) This goggle-eyed fish's eyes make it easier to see at night.

A male fairy basslet (top) can control harems of smaller orange-yellow females. If the male dies or is killed, one of the females (bottom) changes sex to replace the missing male.

What happens when the male fairy basslet gets sick and dies or is devoured by another hungry fish? If there aren't enough males, one of the females simply changes its sex to become the new male. Not only does the former female fish take on the distinctive markings of a male, it can also produce the sperm necessary to fertilize the females' eggs!

FISHES OF THE RED SEA: Self-Protection

Partnerships or alliances don't occur only between members of the same species of animal. Another way fishes can improve their chances of survival is to form alliances with different kinds of animals in the sea. In the case of the clownfish and the anemone, both partners probably benefit.

Embedded in the gently waving tentacles of the flowery anemone are thousands of coiled, flexible harpoons. Called nematocysts, these poisonous harpoons are simply waiting to explode if their tentacles are so much as touched. The barbed missiles launched by some of the more powerful anemones are strong enough to paralyze or kill a careless fish.

Mysteriously—through a process scientists still don't completely understand—clownfishes can disarm the anemone so its arrows are never fired. Clownfishes coat their own bodies with a special mucous. When the anemone's tentacles touch the specially coated fish, they do not recognize the fish as an intruder.

The clownfish thus has a private preserve among the tentacles. Some biologists feel the anemone benefits by getting an occasional free meal carried in by a scavenging clownfish. Clownfish also do a good job of chasing butterflyfish away; some butterflyfish are able to nibble the anemones' tentacle tips and survive, something scientists can't explain.

Sometimes alliances between fishes aren't protection enough and some serious self-advertisement is called for. What about all those brightly colored fishes and invertebrates that appear in broad daylight? Aren't they inviting their own destruction? While animals such as the yellow and black nudibranch (sea slug or shell-less snail) don't usually try to show off during the day, whenever they do come out of hiding, their colors signal a warning to other predators. Certain color combinations are recognized in the animal world as meaning that their wearers are poisonous or foul tasting.

The yellow and black sea slug is the underwater equivalent of the bumble bee. And the bright red color of another sea slug, the Spanish dancer, probably carries this warning as well. But just in case a hungry animal comes around that doesn't understand its message, the Spanish dancer has another trick in store. By wriggling its body, this gorgeously colored nudibranch dances up into the water currents for a swim to a safer place.

The Moses sole brings self-protection to even more powerful extremes. The sole is a flatfish or flounder, and its shape lends itself well to the game of hide and seek. The thin body blends in nicely with the floor of the sea. Like a chameleon, the sole can match the color of its surroundings. But survival in the Red Sea apparently demands even more from its fishes. Some clever detective work by fish biologist Eugenie Clark, who was investigating the Moses sole, revealed an interesting story. During her frequent dives in the Red Sea, Dr. Clark noticed how fishes of all shapes and sizes kept their distance from the Moses sole. Experiments to see if *any* animal would eat the seemingly harmless flatfish produced an even bigger surprise. The fluid that oozed from the base of its fins was so poisonous that even the mightiest of sharks left it alone.

The Moses sole is one of a host of undersea animals that live or hide in the sand. Brush aside the coral rubble at the base of a reef, and you may find a pair of ghoulish eyes. The security of the sand is important to some of the Red Sea's fishes. At night many wrasses hide and sleep covered by coral sand. The natural camouflage of a crocodilefish allows it to lie in the sand undetected, and then pounce on food day or night. And you can be certain another kind of fish called the stargazer isn't simply staring at the stars.

(Facing page) The Red Sea clownfish finds safety and protection among the stinging tentacles of an anemone. Most other fishes that try only get jabbed by the anemone's stinging barbs.

A milky fluid from a flatfish called the Moses sole is so poisonous that most fishes, including sharks, stay away.

(Facing page) Shell-less snails called nudibranchs are called the butterflies of the sea. To defend their soft bodies, the Spanish dancer (top left) can swim out of danger. Other nudibranchs, such as the black, white, and yellow varieties, discourage predators with their unpleasant taste.

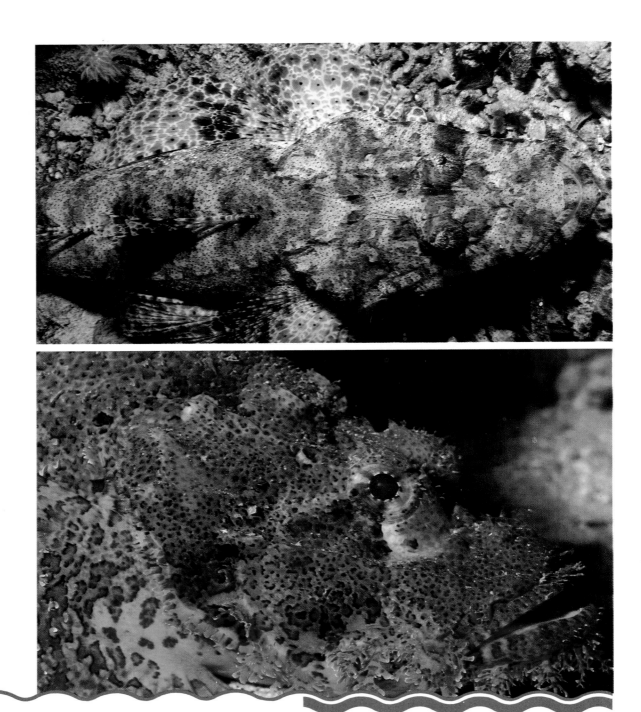

A crocodilefish (top) and a scorpionfish use color and beardlike fringes to hide against the background of the coral reef. Can you tell the crocodilefish apart from its surroundings?

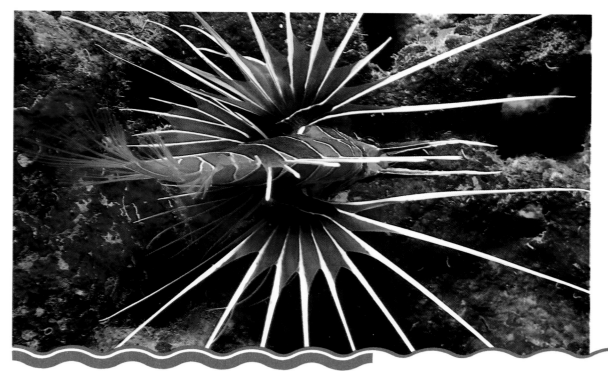

The turkey- or zebrafish doesn't change colors like other scorpionfishes. But it does protect itself with spines that contain venom.

Some stargazers are a kind of living battery. Hidden in a pouch behind each eye are special electric organs that can deliver a fifty-volt shock. That's almost half the electricity delivered to household outlets, and it's certainly enough to shock many fishes into submission. It also creates an invisible electric field all around the stargazer's body. If another fish swims by, an alarm system is triggered by the stargazer's electric eye. Even if an intruder gets past its electric shield, there are some varieties of stargazers around the world that add to their arsenal with powerful, venomous spines.

Although its venom is not as powerful as the deadly stonefish, an encounter with the scorpionfish cannot be considered lightly. Hovering in midwater or sitting motionless on the reef floor, an aroused scorpionfish will point a quiver of spines at an inquisitive intruder. Pierced by these spines, fish or diver alike will feel agonizing pain caused by the venom it injects from glands at the base of its fins.

PRESERVING THE RED SEA FOR THE FUTURE

The Red Sea today is a rare and unusual place, as special as the continent of Antarctica, the rain forests of Brazil, the Galápagos Islands, and Australia's Great Barrier Reef. So far, it has survived the heat of its deserts, the wars between its neighboring states, and an endless parade of oil supertankers that pass through the Suez Canal. But oil, sewage, and overfishing threaten the Red Sea's coral reefs. The Gulf of Suez, for example, is one of the most rapidly developing offshore oil-drilling areas in the world. Oil and sewage clog the seaside mangrove forests which, like salt marshes, are nurseries to the reef's juvenile fishes. Chemicals coat the tiny coral animals so they can't eat or reproduce. Overfishing robs the reef of adults so that not enough young are produced. But despite all of these threats, there are beginning to be more promising signs.

Among the disturbing signs of environmental abuse is some encouraging news. The countries that border the Red Sea—Israel, Egypt, Jordan, Sudan, Ethiopia, Saudi Arabia, Djibouti, and Yemen—are making a new commitment. Of these eight modern nations, most have at least begun plans to protect the Red Sea wildlife in areas they control. Based on Israel's lead, a network of major marine parks may eventually preserve the Red Sea's underwater riches for all generations to come.

(Facing page) A brightly striped triggerfish (foreground) and a coral grouper peer out from a background of soft coral colors.

Glossary

algae (AL-jee)—an enormous variety of plantlike organisms that live mostly in fresh or salt water, ranging from microscopic single cells to large seaweeds one hundred feet (30.5m) long

bioluminescence (by-oh-loo-muh-NES-ens)—a chemical process in some living organisms that produces light

calcium (CAL-see-um)—a silver-white metallic element found in chalk, marble, and limestone

coral reef (KOR-ul-REEF)—a huge natural formation built up of the abandoned limestone skeletons of coral animals found only in tropical waters

cowrie (COW-ree)—a tropical sea snail with a long narrow opening bordered by small toothlike projections

crown-of-thorns sea star—a tropical sea star that eats coral animals

flashlight fish—fishes of tropical oceans or seas that use light-emitting organs below their eyes to attract food, confuse predators, and find mates

Gulf of Aqaba (AK-uh-buh)—northeasternmost gulf of the Red Sea, ending at the border of Israel

Gulf of Suez (soo-EZ)—northwesternmost gulf of the Red Sea, joining the Mediterranean Sea through the Suez Canal

hard, or stony, corals (KOR-uls)—animals that create solid skeletons of limestone (calcium carbonate), forming the foundation of a coral reef

harem (HAR-um)—a group of female animals dominated by a single male

killifish (KIL-i-fish)—a family of generally small fishes, including the desert pupfish and the common mummichog of the Atlantic coast

limestone (LIME-stone)—rock, mainly calcium carbonate, formed chiefly from the remains of certain marine animals

nematocysts (NEM-ut-uh-sists)—stinging cells that form thousands of coiled, flexible stingers in the tentacles of anemones and other invertebrates; the stingers are released like harpoons into their prey

nudibranch (NOOD-uh-brank)—a type of carnivorous marine snail which has a shell only in its larval stage

polyp (POL-up)—a stage in the lives of jellyfishes, sea anemones, and corals consisting of a simple stomach with a mouth surrounded by tentacles

predator (PRED-uh-tur)—an animal that kills other animals for food

sea fans—soft corals that form flat, branching structures

sea whips—soft corals that form long filaments, usually somewhat curved at the ends

soft corals—corals like sea fans and sea plumes with flexible skeletons that can bend in water currents and capture plankton as food

tapetum (tah-PEET-um)—a membrane at the back of the eyes of certain animals that reflects light through the retina and increases vision in dim light

tentacles (TENT-ih-kuhls)—long, flexible structures, usually on an animal's head or around its mouth, used for grasping, stinging, or sensing

territory—an area that animals defend as their personal space against the threat of other animals

zooplankton (zoh-uh-PLANK-ton)—free-floating, often microscopic animals that live in water and are transported largely by water currents

zooxanthellae (zoh-uh-zan-THEL-ee)—microscopic algae that live inside the tissues of coral animals. Like the leaves of trees, the algae use the energy of sunlight to make food, which helps nourish the coral.

Bibliography

Bemert, Gunnar. *Red Sea Coral Reefs.* London and Boston: Kegan Paul International, 1981.

Clark, E. "Life in an Undersea Desert." *National Geographic Magazine,* vol. 164, no. 1, July 1983: 129—131.

Edwards, A. and S. Head. *Key Environments, Red Sea.* Oxford: Pergamon Press, published in collaboration with the International Union for Conservation of Nature and Natural Resources, 1988.

Fishelson, Lev, and David Pilosof. *Mysteries of the Red Sea.* Dobbs Ferry, New York: Sheridan House, Inc., 1984.

Jacobs, Francine. *The Red Sea.* New York: Morrow, 1981.

Levine, J. *Undersea Life.* New York: Tabori & Chang, 1985.

Randall, J. *Red Sea Reef Fishes,* 36—43, 52—3, 55, 85, 87, 104, 112, 126—9, 135—142. London: IMMEL Publishing, 1983, reprint 1986.

Vine, P. *Red Sea Invertebrates,* 7—8, 33—50, 53—80, 145—155, 192. London: IMMEL Publishing, 1986.

Index

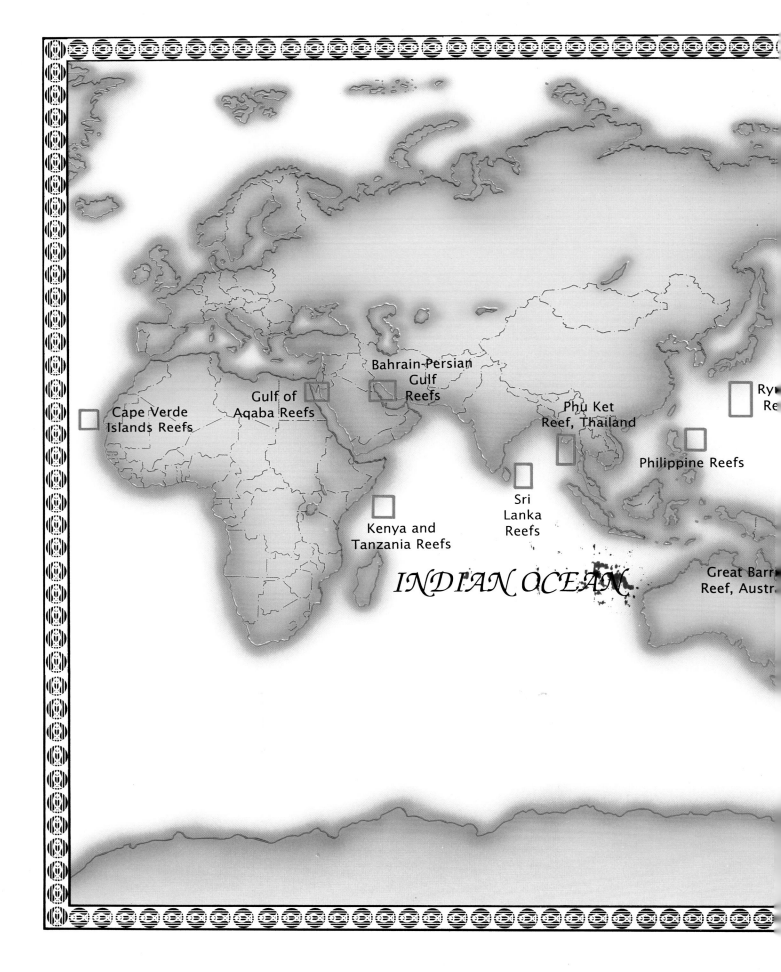

Cape Verde
Islands Reefs

Gulf of
Aqaba Reefs

Bahrain-Persian
Gulf
Reefs

Ry◄
Re

Phu Ket
Reef, Thailand

Philippine Reefs

Kenya and
Tanzania Reefs

Sri
Lanka
Reefs

INDIAN OCEAN

Great Barr
Reef, Austr